SELECTED POEMS

by

Elizabeth Daryush

from Verses I-VI

ERRATA

Poem 1	line 8	for *high* read *stern*
Poem 6	line 12	for *ecstasy.* read *ecstasy."*
Poem 21	line 6	for *Nor* read *No.*
Poem 36	line 6	for *well-know* read *well-known*
Poem 48	line 9	for *night's calm* read *night-calm*
Poem 65	line 8	for *My* read *With*
Poem 75	line 1	for *they* read *thy*

SBN 902145 77 0

First published 1972
by Carcanet Press Ltd.
Pin Farm South Hinksey Oxford

CONTENTS

39	I know	III
40	Fresh Spring, in whose	III
41	You who to the copse	I
42	I led into the silent room	II
43	Farewell for a while	III
44	As, those hours of sorrow ended	I
45	Harebell of the idle hill	III
46	You should at times go out	IV
47	If your loved one	IV
48	Today was the drear song	II
49	Throstle in the wood	VI
50	If you were not what I know	IV
51	Is this then grandeur	VI
52	Anger, last enemy	VI
53	How long, said spirit	II
54	I sought, sought for my sweet	IV
55	Suspense has drained	L. M.
56	O strong to bless	I
57	Alone with staring thought	L. M.
58	Sunless November	II
59	Christmas eve – a scene	VI
60	Of whom if not of these	L. M.
61	From day to converse night	II
62	Once more, brave morning	II
63	Fear not lest the morrow bring	II
64	The lily said	I
65	I will hold out my arms	II
66	Ten years, perhaps, or twenty	L. M.
67	Well, and what of it?	IV
68	It is pleasant to hang out	IV
69	The woman I'd revere	IV
70	A squalid July street	VI
71	Eyes that queenly sit	III
72	When your work's done	L. M.
73	What though many praise me	II
74	The wide road from the city	II
75	Tell not they trouble	II
76	Beyond the firs	L. M.
77	We have seen endangered ships	II
78	Here, where the larks sing	IV
79	Wherefore solicit	IV
80	Wild thoughts anon	II
81	Once more, light bringer	I
82	Plant no poppy	III
83	For my misdeed	IV

NOTE

This book contains virtually all that I wish to preserve from the following publications: *Verses* (1930); *Verses, Second Book* (1932); *Verses, Third Book* (1933); *Verses, Fourth Book* (1934); *The Lost Man & Other Verses* (1936) – all published by the Oxford University Press; and *Verses, Sixth Book* (1938), which I published myself. Many of the poems have been revised, and one or two largely rewritten. Nothing is here included from a later book, *Verses, Seventh Book* 1971, which is published by the Carcanet Press. (Three early books, written before 1922, I have already suppressed.)

As usual, the poems in syllabic metres are distinguished by the absence of line-capitals.

E.D.

I made this garden, this heav'n of sight,
said the artist, I planned every bed
of beauty-hues, of fadeless delight.

I raised these woods, the musician said,
these lofty strains; I turned the bare ground
to groves celestial of noble sound.

But he whose paints are only rich words,
his tunes but twining thoughts, said: These grew,
these vines, I see not how, though upwards

I trained or pruned them as best I knew;
where gladness shone, where sorrow's stream flowed,
I found them, and beside the worn road.

1

Life, a tree of toil I plant thee;
Only thus to grow I'll grant thee:

Wax in sombre strength, devouring
All my plots of pleasant flowering:

Soar in resolution, slaying
All my lawns of small displaying:

Branch in ardour self-transcending:
Surpass even thy high intending:

From thy root if nothing shake thee,
Then, though Time the woodman break thee,
He'll for Beauty's building take thee.

2

Now the beauteous lamps are low:
Who'll stand forth, fair light to show?
I will, said the voice I know.

Who'll be for benighted man
A torch in his army's van?
I will, said he, *for I can.*

Who can his whole being fill
With fire, till that fire him kill?
I, said he, *if God so will.*

3
PERSIAN DAWN

The air is light; the rustling leaves
   Of the tall planes remember not
Nor the loud jays, how yestereve's
   Oppression hung, a burden hot:

The village street knows naught amiss,
   The chattering workers go their ways,
As though they too forgot how this
   Morn also must, with mounting blaze

Through steep laborious heats lead on
   To noon's fierce summit of distress,
To the grim path whose goal is won,
   At last, of night, of pathlessness.

4

I prayed that on my mortal road
   Endless truth would enlighten me;
The gloom said: "What is this thy God,
   To thus attend and answer thee?"

I said: "The brightest that I know,
   My warmest thought, to this I kneel:
To this in ecstasy I bow,
   To this in anguish I appeal."

The sun rose up in glory strong
   And said: "Behold my heavenly blaze:
'Tis I alone to whom belong
   Thy dawns, thy now so lustrous days:

"'Twas I who from brute mire thy spark
   Created, fanned, till up it strove;
'Twas I who in thy terror dark
   Lit for thee faith and hope and love:

"'Twas I alone who, lulling thee,
   In rhythms did thy life arrange,
Who then to thought continually
   Quickened thee with the varying change

"Of hour and month and season fair" –
   I murmured: "Yes; and yet, I know
That past this warmly pulsing sphere
   Surges infinity's cold flow

"Of forces that no flesh can chart,
  Where life, if any life there be,
Is alien to my human heart,
  Is naught that can companion me;

"I know that in that ocean blent
  Of time with triple-brinkéd space,
All the primeval firmament
  Is but a point, an instant's place,

"A fleck of foam that in some thrall
  Is gripped a moment and is gone –
A droplet is the earth, and all
  The lucent film of life thereon,

"A mote that through some mighty beam
  Of stress is drawn, and thus is lit
To life, to love, that so must seem
  To us the force that fashioned it,

"For we, the breakings of that strain
  In the unknown, are not till dim power's
O'ercharge – its urge of lifeless pain
  Ends in the pain-flash that is ours,

"In lightnings fierce of passionate need,
  Of eager giving . . . When again
Shall vivid wish and word and deed
  Vanish, burnt out, what then, what then?" . . .

The rocket of man's reaching thought
    Soars, soars, then quivers, pauses, breaks
In coloured stars: the mind distraught
    In fading sparks, in art-fire speaks.

5

AFTER BANK HOLIDAY

Now deserted are the roads
   Where awhile the lovers went;
Vacant are the field-abodes
   Where a vivid hour they spent:
      Solemn dark
   Broods again in lane and park.

'Tis no matter where are gone
   Those warm lives – to halls, maybe,
Festive, or to lodgings lone:
   Of the land their tenancy
      Now is o'er;
   Earth to earth belongs once more.

Gone are they as hourly goes
   From the sombre fields of space
Our world, with its little glows–
   Passion's ship that has no place
      On the track
   O'er time's endless ocean black.

6

Mortality, and her drear daughter, Age –
Mortality, that holds my joy's brief book,
Presenting slowly every ordered page,
Then turning it, ere I enough can look;
Stern-meting Age, filler of pleasure's glass,
Who ever subtler, paler wine must pour,
Richer, maybe, but, as the swift years pass,
Ever less sweet, till used be all my store –

O, there's no glory in the glowing day,
No splendour in the shining night, but she
Will whisper: "This is passing soon for aye";
Or she: "I'll give no more this ecstasy.

"Crush I forever now this leaf." "This flask
I break: for this again thou shalt not ask."

7
INVALID DAWN

Above the grey down
   gather, wan, the glows;
relieved by leaden
   gleams a star-gang goes;

in the dark valley
   here and there enters
a spark, laggardly,
   to the faint watchers

that were there all night –
   factory, station
and hospital light. . . .
   Tired of lamp, star, sun,

bound to my strait bed
   uncurtained, I see
heaven itself law-led,
   earth in slavery.

8

Once more
The sea of Winter breaks upon a waveless shore;
I hear a sound
Of rippling (as of bird-song) over sunny ground;

Again
The tide of icy darkness, of starvation-bane,
Has turned to bring
Our ship to the warm cliffs (like orchards white) of Spring,

Where soon
The mariners will land, as they have often done,
Whistling the while,
Impatient to explore another summer-isle,

To know
This one, too, of the endless archipelago –
Gladly, once more,
Have they forgot their charter, with its term obscure.

9

Seeing the company of Spring I say:
O, would that my words could command alway
The fair ones camping in my field today!

Would that I might, when meets she wintry doom,
Call back full-bosomed chestnut, to resume
Her billowy green frock worked with pearly bloom;

Would that I might be summoner of the charms
Of scented may, what time no more she warms
Out-holding to the sun her long white arms,

And lilac heavy-headed, drunk with all
Her fragrant dreaming, and laburnam tall
With her loose amber locks poetical,

And rhododendron, and her sister sweet
Luxurious azalea – where they meet
From gold to carmine is the flame complete,

And curly-headed hyacinth, and vain
Narcissus like a slim boy, in the train
Of amazonian tulip, smartly plain –

Would that I might, glad with immortal skill,
Set here for aye all who awhile now fill
My garden, followers of time's sad will.

10
THE POET AND HIS SEASONS

I have a pact with palmy Spring:
Sweet happiness of whom I sing
Shall sing of me eternally.

I have a sign from Summer proud:
The glory that I've chanted loud
Shall of my fame the furtherer be.

I have an oath from Autumn drear:
Grief that I've mourned for shall endear
To all mankind my memory.

I have a word from wintry bane –
Most mighty terror, thou'lt remain
My monument, who mov'd'st not me.

11

Autumn, dark wanderer halted here once more,
Grave roamer camped again in our light wood,
With garments ragg'd, but rich and gorgeous-hued,
With the same fraying splendours as before –
Autumn, wan soothsayer, worn gipsy wise,
With melancholy look, but bearing bold,
With lean hard limbs careless of warmth or cold,
With dusky face, and gloomed defiant eyes,

You glanced at summer, and she hung her head;
You gazed, and her fresh cheek with fever burned;
You sighed, and from her flowery vales she turned;
You whispered, and from her fond home she fled:

Now seated by your tattered tent she broods
On timeless heights, eternal solitudes.

12
SONG

THROW AWAY THE FLOWERS

Throw away the flowers,
  they are no use,
  the faery bowers
of the former truce;
    fancy quickly dies
    under fear's dark skies.

Throw away the flowers,
  fetch stubborn rock;
  build for the hours
of terror and shock;
    go to timeless fact
    for what beauty lacked.

Throw away the flowers,
  the tender songs;
  attune your powers
to eternal wrongs;
    have but hopeless, hard
    rebellion for bard.

13
NOVEMBER SUN

His face is pale and shrunk, his shining hair
        Is prison-shorn;
Trailing his grey cloak, up the short dark stair
        He creeps each morn,

Looks out to his lost throne, to the noon-height
        Once his, then turns
Back to the alien dungeon, where all night
        Unseen he burns.

14

Anger lay by me all night long,
  His breath was hot upon my brow,
He told me of my burning wrong,
  All night he talked and would not go.

He stood by me all through the day,
  Struck from my hand the book, the pen;
He said: 'Hear first what *I've* to say,
  And sing, if you've the heart to, *then*.'

And can I cast him from my couch?
  An can I lock him from my room?
Ah no, his honest words are such
  That he's my true-lord, and my doom.

15

I am your lover now, once awful Enmity,
Once strange and gloomy Hate, now I your glory know;
You who erewhile were hell incarnate, now to me
Are heaven, the good for which all others I'll forego –
   Now in imagination that I watch you wreak
   On your own folk the fires that they lit for the weak.

Mildness is no more, Tolerance is done to death,
Pity is buried deep, even Pardon is shut down
Among the shadows, starved of all but ghostly breath;
You alone live, their slaughterer grim, now lovely grown;
   Now could I die for you, who in mad dream I see
   Reversed on your own fiends, O now right enmity!

(After a massacre)

16

Thou say'st: *The clear stream is a troubled river grown . . .*
Would'st then confine it to one field's level alone?

Thou say'st: *The flowery sward is ploughed and heaped with stone . . .*
Would'st then the treed garden's high perfection postpone?

Thou say'st: *The hard woman doth the maiden dethrone . . .*
Would'st rank, O mortal, what's but to heaven's ruler known?

17

What I can's a voice,
kindly, musical,
saying: "Rest, rejoice";

what I cannot, blares
like a trumpet-call
its rousing despairs.

What I can's a flower,
a lush leafy shoot,
very Eden's bower;

what I cannot, glows
like forbidden fruit,
whose wine-juice none knows.

18
LULLABY

Loose the horses now
from harness and plough,
let them plod off, slow,
head bent, stumblingly,
too tired out to see,
to the stall they know.

Follow them not there,
let them lie alone,
they'll be in the care
of a kind mistress,
she knows how to dress
bruiséd flesh and bone,

her simples are good
for soreness and ache,
at dawn they'll be back,
champing, lusty-thewed –
loose the horses now
from harness and plough.

19
SLEEPLESS

'Tis for you to shut the door
of your room against the roar
of sorrow's on-thundering sea;

'tis for you to draw your blown
curtains close before the moon
of beauty that cannot be,

'tis for you to dout the fire,
to stamp on flickering desire . . .
In silence, obscurity,

'tis then for your Mother kind
to bring you the draught, to blind
and deafen your weary mind –
she will come; constant is she.

20

One creature, foul or fair,
What is't for Nature's care?
Her world of want and strife
Teems with contented life.

One spark, or low or higher,
What is't to the whole fire
Of human discontent,
Of lust malevolent?

Yet sainthood beckons thee . . . .
Perish, then, speck apart
From man's fierce-flaming heart;
Die, white bird blown to sea
From earth's sufficiency.

21
MARCH 21

The wood's alive to-day –
   Warm power all round
Breathes like a beast of prey
   Waiting to bound. . . .

It was no timid bird,
   Nor harmless snake,
The rustle that I heard
   In the birch-brake;

It was no fair red bud
   On the larch-bough
That I saw, but drawn blood –
   The warning now

Of bliss that will not bide,
   Of need too full,
Too fierce, to be denied,
   Wild, terrible. . . .

22

I am your mother, your mother's mother,
I am your father, his father also;
look on me, see each living ancestor;
it is well you should understand your kin,
should learn who your body's bound to, should know
who they are whose house you are prisoned in.

I am your dear spouse, your wife, your husband,
I am nearer to you than your own folk,
I am what you loved, freely chose, the friend
you cannot leave – ev'n in the tomb I wait
to be your soul's only companion. . . . Look,
if you dare, on your mind's eternal mate.

(After Jalāl ud Din Rūmi)

23

'Only relief, no less,
Real flesh-relief, no false sublimation. . . .'
To you who clamour thus, quick hour of temptation,
Comes a dumb ghost;
A sister-hour unshriven from the soul's own past
Says with her gaze: 'Ah yes,

I know, I know,
Who once as you suffered, burned with thirst-woe;
I am Persephone,
The sometime fair Hope-maiden, who roamed free
Among the flowers, till Hell's arch-lord, Default,
Swept me down, down, to the dark ante-vault
Where, after long drouths, parchings past belief,
They offered me the pomegranate. . . . I knew
The hard condition, yet I cried, I too,
'Only relief' . . . . Ah (you
Who know) feel, feel now what this one relief
Will mean, whose taking shall destroy your place
In the bright world, shall prison you in gloom,
Shall wed you to remorse. . . . Look on my face,
Friend, I implore you. . . . Guess that lord, that home'. . . .

24
DROUGHT

The shadeless elms, the poplars shimmerless
Have yellowed, dropped their flaccid leaves a full
Two months before their time; the alder-pool
Is a black miry swamp, ploughed by the press
Of tortured, thirsty cattle; or look where
Once would a spreading line of verdure show
The river's lush umbrageous path, that now
Is a hard white road, hedged with willows bare.

Autumn will flush no harvest in these fields
Failed of slow Nature's sober, ripening clime,
Nor winter in these woods brighten with rime
Red berry, brown nut, her late-lavished yields

To bird and beast: the blighted copse they rob
Already of its last lean hip and cob.

25

On the wings unseen
   Of chance's breaths
Borne are we between
   Life's world, or death's:

On the trembling cord
   Of our frail will
Walk 'neath God's high word
   O'er deepest ill;

And through all that parts
   Glad heaven from hell
Quicklier fall our hearts
   Than tongue can tell.

26

Children of wealth in your warm nursery,
Set in the cushioned window-seat to watch
The volleying snow, guarded invisibly
By the clear double pane through which no touch
Untimely penetrates, you cannot tell
What winter means; its cruel truths to you
Are only sound and sight; your citadel
Is safe from feeling, and from knowledge too.

Go down, go out to elemental wrong,
Waste your too round limbs, tan your skin too white;
The glass of comfort, ignorance, seems strong
To-day, and yet perhaps this very night

You'll wake to horror's wrecking fire – your home
Is wired within for this, in every room.

27

The servant-girl sleeps. By the small low bed,
On the mean chest of drawers, are carefully
Arranged her poor belongings – photos spread
Cross-wise, a box of tawdry jewelry. . .
Outside the airless attic looms the vast
Of sultry night; huge clouds are mounting, fraught
With lurid flashes. . . . Look! A tremor passed
Over the tired face, as of anxious thought.

Is it of lightning tragedy she dreams?
Is it of darkly louring pain and care?
What profound unrest to her pent soul seems
To gloom the world? '*On Sunday shall I wear*

The white? . . . It's less becoming . . . but the blue
Is last year's fashion now . . . and faded, too.'

28
STILL-LIFE

Through the open French window the warm sun
lights up the polished breakfast-table, laid
round a bowl of crimson roses, for one –
a service of Worcester porcelain, arrayed
near it a melon, peaches, figs, small hot
rolls in a napkin, fairy rack of toast,
butter in ice, high silver coffee-pot,
and, heaped on a salver, the morning's post.

She comes over the lawn, the young heiress,
from her early walk in her garden-wood
feeling that life's a table set to bless
her delicate desires with all that's good,

that even the unopened future lies
like a love-letter, full of sweet surprise.

29

All that shall ne'er be thine,
  Beauty, maybe, or love,
Wealth, or the power whose wine
  Lifts thee the world above,

Branches whose nectar-fruit
  Thou canst but smell and see,
The flowery Eden-plot
  By fate forbidden thee –

Wan loiterer, beware:
  Thy road unnatural
Is haunted – whispers there
  The subtlest snake of all: –

Thou, with God's chosen few,
  Abjurest poisoned lust:
Thou scorn'st as angels do
  The garland that's but dust.

30
FRUSTRATION

God granted, God denies –
    So faith has said;
But fonder faith still cries
    Uncomforted.

Now are thy labours o'er –
    But hope says: 'These
That make me, love I more
    Than barren ease.'

Still shalt thou glorify
    Thy God – Nay, still
Bends desire but to *my*
    Creating will.

31
BLIND

Patience, the woman that attends on me,
That every morning sweeps my soul's dark room,
Ranges the thought that hangs where light should be,
Prepares for sense its sustenance of gloom –
Patience, the care-taker drear-voiced and sour,
Of ways abstemious, of small wishes few,
The plodding creature that must every hour
Return and rectify whate'er I do –

Patience, that has but one consoling word,
One same grey comfort for my sorrow black,
Mutt'ring the hard text that so oft I've heard:
All highest wealth is won from lowest lack –

She wearies me to death, and yet I know
That for my life I dare not bid her go.

32

You who are blest, say this: 'The canvas blank
That's my free life, the years without one line
Drawn on them of restraint, for which I thank
My God, he gave me that I should design
Bold vivid beauty – should my soul imbrue
In its own blood, kill self – or feel the sword
Of cruellest failure's conquering.' . . . But you,
Curst in pain's prison, say: 'I praise my Lord
That he the sombre plan did not refuse
To limn – has left me but the simpler work
Of filling up the outline, with what hues
I may of sober patience, colours dark

Of courage – that he keeps me from the stress,
The anguished dangers, of unhinderedness.'

33
AMBITION

Another day held out by future's hand,
Another strung on past's assembling thread,
To its eternal place in order led,
A graded pearl upon a necklace planned;
Small were the orbs at first, of value small,
Then slowly waxed, became the precious row
Which, waxing still, must yet ere long, I know
Wane to their worthlessness original.

Another day's work set on the fine cord
Of willed intent, that shall or beauty bring
To clasped completion, or, too frail, shall fling
Away of all my pains the one reward –

The gift that with time's gifts I would create,
To which all thoughts, words, deeds I dedicate.

34

God's light is, to guess
   (where you have not been)
brighter fieriness,

passionately to fight
   till the splendour seen
is your place by right,

to pass on, look back
   at glory . . . discern
only deepest black . . .

Need, fatigue, shame – three
   Hells wherein to burn . . .
   This is toil's return,
   this the heaven we earn
everlastingly.

35

What is a summer day? A century –
More than a life-span – all of golden prime,
Of power, of brilliance, urging, burning me
To save, translate it as immortal rhyme;
It is a continent, from pole to pole
(From mist-white dawn to evening) all the way
A paradise, wherein the scenes unroll
Of warmth, of wonderment too sweet to say.

It is what leads to hours more amorous still,
To dusk's even lovelier gardens, where again,
Like wafts essential that the soul o'er-fill,
Passions seem almost poesy . . . ah then

To the dark paths like naught but death – despair
At light, life, love that I cannot declare.

36
THE ENCHANTRESS

The moon lay on her couch of cloud
   Above the gloomed floor of the land,
Under the darkening arch where glowed
   Now distantly the glory banned. . . .

Veiled was the dais of the downs
   Lost was the well-know line between
The embers of the living towns,
   The star-lamps of where heaven had been,

And she that is nor present love
   Nor memoried, neither flesh nor soul,
Smiled . . . smiled . . . *'The future will I move,*
   Creation's seas will I control'.

37

Have you noticed
The slim buds of the beech, how first they bend
Sun-wards, then, almost visibly, extend
To be warm-kissed
Their finger-fans . . . how soon attain their tender prime
The lucent leaf-throngs that aloft in softness blend? . . .
'Ah, yes, I have a pass to fancy's amorous clime.'

Or has bracken
Shown you, first, proud heads bowed, then a scant band
Of forms strained but ecstatic . . . then, full-manned
Fern-armies, green
Gold, gory? . . . 'Shall no faery strifes attend my state
To whom belongs now every season's passionate land? –
Who therefore stiffly walk, salute nor love nor hate'.

38

O tragic world of dark and stars,
   Of splendours wasted on the void,
Of weary, ever-circling wars,
   Of hopes new-lit and hopes destroyed,

O glorious world of sun and flowers,
   Of passion freed in perfect form,
Of ever-fresh triumphant powers,
   Of living grace, of grandeur warm –

My soul has thrown his window wide,
   And soared into your boundless grief;
My heart has to her garden hied
   And roamed your rapture past belief,

Who now returned to their small room
   Sit talking in the twilight grey –
Wonder: 'Which was the dream? . . . the gloom,
   Then, or the gladness? . . . night or day?'

39

I know
That death's in ambush everywhere I go,
With bow full-bent
To strike my sluggard powers ere they be spent:

I know
That waits he for my loved ones even so,
And, when he'll smite,
Shall stab me too, shall faulty love requite;

Yet still
To mind's affirming, deaf is slothful will:
Still lax and vain
Is heart, nor hears how memory weeps amain.

40

Fresh Spring, in whose deep woods I sought,
   As in your cool abodes I played,
The phantoms of my childish thought,
   The spirits of the faery shade;

Warm Summer, in whose fields I met
   My fancy's every fond device,
Where small imagination set
   The very scenes of Paradise;

Now are your forests high the hall
   Of shades more surely fugitive;
Now raptures lost beyond recall
   In your unsunned recesses live;

Now to your cloudless meadows come
   Forms lit with longing's fiercest flame;
Now truly are your haunts their home
   Eternal, whom with tears I name.

41

BYE-FLOWERS

You who to the copse are gone,
  You who haunt the orchard-rill,
Whose shy graces are outshone
  By the bolder daffodil;

You who near the river's edge
  Stand like modest maidens tall,
Crowded by the ousting sedge,
  Slim waifs of the waterfall;

You who the hard stubble-field
  Have with flaunting poppy shared,
You who make the hedge a shield,
  Blindly by the mower spared;

You who live with the lean grass
  Of the wind-worn, chalky down,
So diminished, that men pass
  Your sweet faces by unknown –

Ah, not lightly may I speak
  Your too well remembered names,
Your once starry beauties seek
  That now like loved living flames

Prick each scene familiar, glow
  Warm as his far look intent,
Who my childhood taught to know
  Your fair hidden firmament.

42

I led into the silent room
   The stranger, waited there
Beside him who for this had come
   From his far hemisphere.

The ordered books, the desk full-strewn,
   The faded curtain green
Tempering the sun of afternoon,
   All was as it had been

But that the air, inhumed and hushed,
   Was of no earthly clime—
I stood, but my claimed spirit rushed
   Back, back o'er seas of time.

I heard the pilgrim's movéd speech,
   My measured speech, as hears
One havened in the past the beach
   Where break rough present's years.

43

Farewell for a while,
My lov'd one, only;
For earth's little mile
Of pathway lonely;

For one weary march
Of sense's pining,
Driv'n out from the arch
Of joy's enshrining;

For one journey short
Of thought's sore bearing,
Expelled from the fort
Of sorrow's sharing;

Till once more the height
Of truth attainéd,
I'll see the lost light
Of love unwanéd,

Where (so longing saith)
Life's road shall leave me –
No more, mortal death,
Shalt thou deceive me.

(*For* M. M. B., *April* 1932.)

44

As, those hours of sorrow ended,
Gave we up – 'twas his desire –
Our loved burden, nor defended
Our faint spirits from the fire,
But in fierce destruction sharing,
Purged our mortal need's despairing,

So, to our changed home returning,
Left we what he bade us leave;
With hearts full, yet not of yearning,
Too exalted now to grieve,
Giving thanks, our tears then stayed we –
So, too, his behest obeyed we.

45
BIRTHDAY BOUQUET

Harebell of the idle hill,
   Cockle of industrious corn,
Meadowsweet of laughing rill,
   Restharrow of heath forlorn,
      Are for her whose quiet face
      Welcome is in every place.

Poppy crimson, scarlet too,
   Marigold whose bluish green
Leads to cornflower's primal blue,
   Scabious, mallow, here shall mean
      Her whose simple spirit white
      Is the sum of all that's bright.

So at end of summer we,
   Gathering symbols for her, say
What with the soul's eye we see;
   So too, now, this prayer will pray –
      That she whom love warmed shall bless,
      Blooming long, our sunlessness.

(For M. M. B., August 31, 1931)

46

You should at times go out
  from where the faithful kneel,
visit the slums of doubt
  and feel what the lost feel;

you should at times walk on,
  away from your friends' ways,
go where the scorned have gone,
  pass beyond blame and praise;

and at times you should quit
  (ah yes) your sunny home,
sadly awhile should sit,
  even, in wrong's dark room,

or ever, suddenly
  by simple bliss betrayed,
you shall be forced to flee,
  unloved, alone, afraid.

47
FOR –

If your loved one prove unworthy, why then,
by this much you're the freer: if the block
to which you're bolted warp and shrink away,
why then, it only gives you further play,
makes life rough for you, of course, with its knock
and rattle, with defection's loud sudden
jars, but your own quiet integrity,
tried thus the more, has but more room to be.

So says one truth, but soon says another:
Now in your soul-tissues a wrong sap stains
the white rose that you were; your heart sustains
the wild-thorn traits of your grafted partner:
when the mistaken marriage mortifies,
it's your own branch and stem and root that dies.

48

Today was the drear song of Nature's mood
        My monody;
The mournful soul of wind and rain and wood
        Was one with me:

Under the straining trees whose tortured power
        Was my pride's own,
I walked the wildered wood-paths, hour on hour,
        By anger blown,

Until with night's calm came fatigue's calm too
        Darkly to bless
Will's stubborn forms; thought's worn ways, fading, knew
        Forgetfulness.

49

Throstle in the wood,
   you know everything
or hurtful or good
   that a lad's feeling;

you know what I feel
   when I bend to take
a sweet cowslip, kneel
   the first, for its sake;

you know what it means
   to find an orchid,
you know what happens
   when whitethorn's sighted;

you know what I know,
   too, of the dárk thorn,
you knew long ago
   before I was born –

throstle in the wood,
   you know everything
or painful or good
   of a lover's Spring.

50
FORBIDDEN LOVE

(For Constance)

If you were not what I know you to be,
(my knight) whose tower of control baffles me,
outside whose bolted and defended gates,
wide-eyed but dumb, my wistful spirit waits,
as a mourner waits by a rock-sealed tomb
for one who comes not, nor can ever come;

if you did not as you do – if you came,
sallied out only a little, to claim
what you know is yours – then it would be I,
(as *I* know that *you* know) who'd fortify
perforce my dwelling, dart sternness at you,
fight you as now I have no need to do.

Were *your* love other than it is, and *my*
love other, they would either force or fly
the deadlock, and, so doing, each would kill
the other, that now from firm walls of will
look friendly, calmly, unafraid to face
even each other, from that high, safe place.

51

Is this then grandeur, says the sun –
To look down on the dwindled world
Whose tiny high and low are one?

Is this then radiance – to be furled
In small earth-urging rounds, to bend
My beams to things that I transcend?

Is this sublimity – to rule
Among soulless inferiors,
Myself but of myself the tool,

Unsummoned by diviner spheres –
To fire *me*, draw *me* there is none –
Is this all heaven then, says the sun?

52

Anger, last enemy,
That the long fight has but increased, not killed,
Fiend racking, piercing me
With thoughts of life's morn-promise unfulfilled,

Night-mood that first I knew
As a mere dusk that dulled my sunny dreams,
Then, ever deepening, grew
To glooms unfathomed, stabbed with passionate gleams,

Ah, how can a soul slay
(Nor slay, too, love itself) your lust love-driven?
How end your hell, nor say:
"You too are naught, all zeal's high starry heaven"?

53

How long, said spirit, must I walk this earth?
I, wingéd, to whom Paradise gave birth,
how long must I pace fields of drought and dearth?

How long, said mind, must I tread the small maze
of paths bewild'ring, of thought that betrays
my straight endeavour with blind-alleyed ways?

How long must I, said life, said bodied soul,
be baulked by faulty flesh from beauty's goal?
How long have but pittance, who see joy's whole?

How long, said heart, may I love's raiment wear?
How long may I work for those I hold dear?
When must I leave them in sorrow and fear?

54

I sought, sought for my sweet–
   She cannot be here,
I found but her void seat
   And her empty lair;

I called, called for my love–
   She must be away,
Silent is her cool grove
   And her garden gay.

With straining eyes I've sought,
   I've heark'd with strain'd ears,
As one with doubts distraught,
   One fevered with fears,

As one who shudd'ring drinks
   But half bitter truth,
As one who sips, then shrinks
   From sharp, scalding ruth,

As one who sorrow sees
   But in fancy hides,
Who the wrecked present flees,
   In the past abides.

55

Suspense has drained all savour from these hours . . .
The fierce sun, poised above our fevered clime
(Moving but imperceptibly as time
Forces it on) still from its filled sky glowers
Insatiate, parches fragrant blooms to dust,
Sucks the sap even from thorns, thirstily kills
All flesh but serpents' – our soft life distils
Of formed desires into one boundless lust.

Travellers of earth's worst desert we toil on,
Worn tough, narrowed by torments to endure
All that once seemed too much for us, and more.
Pleasure, love, beauty are a palmy town

Beyound our grim horizon . . . we forget
Their sunset-land . . . our anguish will not set.

56

O strong to bless
human misery,
sweet lovingkindness
comfort thou me:

thou who alone
mortal hurt canst heal,
most merciful one
to thee I kneel.

Though man may set
his soul to harsh ill,
despising thee, yet
thou lovest still:

yea, though he spurn
thee, leave thee, yet thou
patient, his return
awaitest – now

to us, heart-sore,
solace give; now we,
Mother, yet once more
come home to thee.

57

Alone with staring thought
   I watched the white clouds fly,
I saw what morn had brought
   Pass from the darkening sky.

Alone with my last friend
   I watched the visions fade,
I saw life's sun descend
   Into a soul-less shade.

58

Sunless November, how hast thou now turned
To drear appraisement all our glad employ!
Chill visitor, who com'st but to destroy
With one sad look our summer-wealth late earned
Of glorious bloom; silent remembrancer,
Who, hand on lip, with haunting eye dost tell
To hill and field and wood what know they well –
How changéd shall they be from what they were.

Now, taught beyond her leafy joys, each tree
Lets fall those first that were the first to grow,
Dulling thy steps, as by each dank hedgerow
Of perished grace thou walk'st: now echoes thee
Down the dim alleys of each mind the slow
The muffled footfall of eternity.

59

MODERN CAROL

Christmas eve – a scene
of hoar-gleams and snow . . .
What does whiteness mean?
What does winter show?

Come into the woods,
see the wonder-change;
on everything broods
   a beauty strange;

every twig is soft
   and furred with light,
every bud a tuft
   of feathers bright,

every branch is thick
   and crystal-mossed –
this is the magic
   of fog and frost;

when the heavens are dank,
   the lands icy,
earth is on the brink
of a mystery. . . .

Glory will not last,
peace is only snow,
look at the dark past,
force feeling to know;

faith's a dripping tree,
wonder melts away,
this is what you see,
what you dare not say. . . .

For us who are tired
with truth-light, with cold
now the day, pale-fired,
    ends as of old;

like numbed things that creep
    under dead leaves,
    let us sleep, sleep,
lost to all that grieves,

hid from hard winter's
sun white as a moon,
far from midnight fears
and madness of noon,

safe from beauty's scene,
its hoar-gleams and snow –
from all that has been,
is, shall be, of woe.

60

Of whom if not of these, then, should I sing?
To whom but these hold up the altering glass
Wherein (for so we nature can surpass)
I may create their happier imaging?
To whom, if not to those unlovely ones,
Will's lawless host, dark angels who through pride,
Through aspiration too instant to hide,
Are fall'n for ever, damned with him who shuns
Obedient Heav'n, as him by self's disease
Blemished, deformed, powerless now but to turn
Others likewise to what for aye must burn
In its own Hell . . . . To whom if not to these?

For temperance – all that's devoutly strong –
Needs no art, is its own celestial song.

61

From day to converse night, from night to day,
Often I've turned, not as from dark to light,
But as from glory of day to peace of night,
From drear of night to noon's tormenting ray;
Till know I not from which I now should pray
For rescue, strenuous plight or stagnant plight,
Nor whether angry right or easy right
Be better, how to balance way with way.

Helper there's none on the all-risking road,
For heaven's own gambler there's nor guard nor guide:
No rest is there, save for him who can hide
In his own grey dispassion's tent-abode;
No rapture but for him who wills to ride
The fiery steed that's but on zeal bestowed.

62

Once more, brave morning, bring'st thou here
The shining shield, the new-whet spear:
Once more I take refreshed from thee
My life's familiar armoury.

Once more with bright eyes I behold
The bloomy mist on mountains old,
With eagerness restored I gaze
Where duly thou'lt the curtain raise

On fate's laid scene: nor the cord slips
From thy sure grasp, nor move thy lips,
But in thine endless look is all
That has befall'n, that shall befall.

63

Fear not lest the morrow bring
On her wild-imagined wing
Storms to spoil thy harvesting:

Fear not lest she fail to throw
Beams propitious, who the bow
Did of lofty promise show:

Fear not, though thou never wield
Fame's low sickle: fair's thy yield,
Thou that till'st in faith thy field.

64

The lily said: I labour not to know
What wonders may be in the world beyond;
I look but where my lord has planted me . . .

I care not from what sources strange may flow
The streams that feed me, what mysterious bond
Has solemn rain, or soft dew-alchemy;

Nor in what glooms are quickening airs begun,
What charter has the Spring breeze, or the strong
Warm Summer-breath that now about me stirs;

Enough that on my beauty beauty's sun
Looks every day more ardently, more long,
Saying: "What sweetness is arrayed like hers?"

Low spoke she, meekly bending. In the press
Half hid she was, of lilies numberless.

65

I will hold out my arms
  To spring who clothes me
    (Says the beech),
To kind summer who warms
  My room and soothes me;
    I will reach
For rich autumn's robe, red
  My pride and grieving;
    I will hold
Out my worn dress for dread
  Winter's unweaving
    In the cold.

66

Ten years, perhaps, or twenty – at the most
Less than two score – shall surely terminate
Your lease of Eden, and unloving fate
Shall launch you forth from the enchanted coast. . . .
Is this your lot? One brief hour more of ease,
A garden-walk foreshortened now by fear,
Its forms and odours torturingly dear
To you whose long home is the lifeless seas,

Or this? – An age of struggle on the slope
Of failure's pit, that's deep as the sublime
Cliff's high of what you've set yourself, a time
When naught is real save rock and axe and rope,

And the kind angel-voice that cries at last:
"Rest, for the perils of ascent are passed."

67
FOR –

Well, and what of it? What if you are beautiful?
What if your ready mirror show you hour by hour
far eyes profound as a heaven-reflecting pool,
mouth like the rainbow's smile upon the summer
  shower?
What if your faithful thirsty lovers think of you
as of some draught celestial, some pure passion's wine,
when still the man-made Grail of their adoring view
flows but with vanity, ferment of worldly vine?

Is this achievement? Is this what shall make you glad?
Is this a gift for others bought with your life-blood,
a sweet truth that shall warm men's starving hearts,
  shall add
to weal, this cold, corroding misuse of rich good?

Out on you, woman: quit your beauty, ere the day
when what's within it shall have eat'n it all away.

68
FOR –

It is pleasant to hang out
this sign at your open gate:
"Succour for the desolate" –
your neighbours praise you, no doubt;

but woe to whoe'er in need
at the inner door has knocked,
found the snug room barred and locked
where alone you fatly feed.

69

The woman I'd revere
would be a warm hearth-fire,
not a chilly taper
posed for all to admire,
    a white saint in the gloom,
    but the heart of a home,

a soul burning to bless
its circle, spent for cheer,
a life-giver, thoughtless
how its own life appear,
    whether itself may seem
    a fair or formless gleam.

And the man I'd love, too,
though he'd be a sure light
in the house, a help through
the things of trouble's night,
    would be more than a tame
    measured glow without flame,

one who'd be now and then
o'ercharged with primal power,
a sudden, a rushing
flash in oppression's hour,
    wrath's lightning, rightly hurled,
    the dread of wrong's dark world.

70
THE WARDEN'S DAUGHTER

A squalid July street, a sweaty crowd,
Shop-staring, jostling . . . . That was the mean frame,
The picture, this – a girl whose bearing showed,
Like a cool background, all from whence she came,
Her spacious, quiet home . . . . A coarse, wide hat,
Black-ribboned, cast in shade the exquisite
Pale profile, frail beside the massive plait,
Waist-long, of flaxen glory gathered tight.

I thought: 'Such beauty were a magic boat
Whereby a woman's heart might make its truce
With fate, idly, in its own bliss afloat' –
Forgot how even as honour has no use

For honours, beauty, too, that's of the mind
Sees only tasks, is to its mirror blind.

71

Eyes that queenly sit
   At their casement wide,
Mouth that holdeth it
   As a sentry tried,

For the rest, the face
   Howso built it be,
'Tis the fair palace
   Of fair majesty.

Be the friendly house
   Castle high or cot,
Mean or sumptuous,
   Spirit careth not,

If but strength shall show
   At the guarded gate;
If but the window
   Love illuminate.

72

When your work's done, banish it behind you,
forget its beauties and its failures both;
you've done your part by the child, borne, bred it,
given it your blood, at your heart fed it,
clothed it with care, taught it your hard-learned truth;
now that it's grown let nothing remind you
of what's for ever made lovely, or marred—
no, turn to what's still in your power to guard.

Visit not often the past that bore you,
nor the too-friendly pleasures at your gate,
nor your soul's offspring wedded to their fate—
keep your house, the every need procure you

of those to come, your works yet to be born;
toil, plan and pray for them noon, night and morn.

73

What though many praise me
    for my imperfect song?
They'll only deafen me
    to the notes that are wrong.

What though a few, fondly,
    weave me a garland rare?
I'll sing but drowsily
    in the scent-laden air.

What though my heart even
    whisper at length: "Well done!" –
God grant I'll drink not then
    thy wine, fell poisoning one!

74

ST NICHOLAS

(Isle of Thanet)

The wide road from the city runs
        A furlong from her doors,
And every hurrying tradesman shuns
        Her track unkempt, ignores

The old bleak hamlet, that apart
        Lives her enduring days,
Whose blunt flint tower, uncouth and swart,
        Nor storm nor time decays.

Above her nettly gardens still
        Her knotted elms oppose
Gales whose ungovernable will
        The trim town never knows,

And past her meagre fields the blanked
        (The viewless) distance tells
Where, fronting ocean's roar, are ranked
        Her cliffs' dumb sentinels.

75

Tell not they trouble to that child, the morn,
For she'll to folly win thee unawares;
Nor to noon's amazon who hotly dares,
And thy cool sanity will swift suborn;
Nor to the nun whose ardours quenched are sworn
To twilight peace, nor to her who impairs
More than they all, with her black, blank despairs,
Celestial truth, and leaves thy world forlorn.

Nay; to no mortal hour of gloom or glee
Incline thee; yet awhile let each one look
On what's to hand; their admonitions brook,
Give ear awhile to every plaint and plea:
Forget then feeling's counsellors; turn thee
To thine own place; write all in wisdom's book.

76
WINTER LARCHES

Beyond the firs thick-curtained from the blast,
that hoard in their close unlit house a few
half-rotted cones, brown rags of bracken—past
the draughty ruins of the oaks, that strew
their dank drear courts with wreckage, past the cold
unroofed aisles of the beeches, see how here
the larches standing on their sober gold—
the slow-shed beauty that they wrought and share—
live without shadows in the sunny place
that's of their own making, and a moonlight
of silver lichen on each column's face
shows where it met, scarce moving and upright,

the worst winds . . . Yes, strange timeless beams illume
these halls; here we forget November gloom.

77
SEA-GULLS

We have seen endangered ships
   Driven by the hounding blast,
Rushing from the tooth that strips
   Canvas racked from lurching mast . . . . .
      On the cradling waves we rest:
      Borne are we on safety's breast.

We have watched their progress slow
   When the deadly calm prevailed,
When they grappled with the foe
   Step by short step, heavy-sailed . . . . .
      We have watched from where we ride
      Curvetting, on aery tide.

78

Here, where the larks sing, and the sun's so warm
That gorse-pods click each minute, and the grass
Rustles, as through dry bents the breezes pass,
And butterflies over the heather swarm,
Here I, an ardent lover of all these,
Would build our home – I'd take but the small crest
Of the long hill, and leave untouched the rest,
The coney-shaven turf, the scanty trees.

Here, having marked and worked our cottage-claim,
We'd meet the first shy rays, on summer dawns,
Approaching to unveil our dewy lawns
Of wild-flowers; and when winter evenings came,

We'd watch from our bright room the stealthy dark
Muffling the stunt thorns of our snowy park.

79

Wherefore solicit
  for your daily bread?
The day will bring it,
  will the table spread

that gives ere you ask
  all you need, no less,
to perform your task
  of hard forgiveness.

A morsel of good,
  a dole too of wrong,
is the simple food
  that makes mercy strong;

of joy a small sip,
  of trouble a share,
is all that friendship
  takes to make her fair.

80
EXILE

Wild thoughts that once would fly like homing birds
To a far place, I've caught and tamed you now,
Nor struggle ye more 'gainst my caging words,
But ever meeker, more accustomed grow;
Now are ye hooded hawks whose eager eyes
See only their hard lord's intended prey,
Nor ever for themselves hunt out a prize,
Nor back to their own native region stray.

Here, as there, with a swing of golden doors,
Dawn shall invite to day's long dusty road;
Here, full as comfortingly, dusk restores
Tired flesh in her all-welcoming abode;

Here, too, may needy spirit find again
Cheer's morn, mercy's night, in the hearts of men.

81
SPRING

Once more, light-bringer,
    with unfailing brand,
wake your worshipper
    to understand;

though in the shadow
    winter's haunting near,
on the bright meadow
    falls not a fear;

in the warm wood now
    between grief and grief
blithe is every bough
    and every leaf;

though death's behind me,
    death not far before,
undying beauty
    is at my door.

82

Plant no poppy (he said)
no frail lily sublime,
for in war's famine-time
thou'lt need but corn for bread.

Hoard no jewel (he cried)
no dazzling laboured gem:
thou'lt be forced to sell them
for steel, so now decide.

Set no flower in thy word
(he besought, but none heard)
cut no flash to thy wit,
if thou must disown it
when seest thou sorrow's sword.

83

For my misdeed I blame my erring friend's
No faultier imperfection; so too he
Thrusts back the taunt on one who in turn sends
It farther still; then fancy, winging free,
Bears it on, till, beyond earth's blackened past,
On blameless power primordial lies the blame,
Till on eternal shores my times are cast,
And glory immortal heaped with mortal shame.

Then says the angel, says the ardent soul
That stands above me: "Is not this then proof,
Impious blasphemer, that the wrong's control
Rests but with thee, – that 'neath thine own low roof

Is born, abides, thy sin? Call then a halt
To visiting of blame: take home thy fault."

84
SEPTEMBER

Now the sun's more tender gaze
        Lingers on the land he leaves,
Gilds with ghostly harvest-haze
        Stubble wan and drooping sheaves;

Now in every hedgerow twine,
        Fiery as a farewell bliss,
Flame-leafed briony, the vine,
        Turned to smoke, of clematis;

Now beside the silent stream
        Loosestrife lights her candle tall;
Now the yellowing aspens seem
        High pyres of a funeral

Where from her low couch the mist
    Rises, sighing like a wraith:
"With thy grieving hast thou kissed
        Thy dear follower to death."

85

Faithless familiars,
        summer friends untrue,
once-dear beguilers,
        now wave ye adieu:

swift warmth and beauty
        who awhile had won
my glad company
        I watch you pass on.

Now the still hearth-fire
        intently gloweth,
now weary desire
        her dwelling knoweth,

now a newly-lit
        lamp afar shall burn,
the roving spirit
        stay her, and return.

86

Long, than a hair more slender, is the bridge
Set for thy saving: from the first high land
Whence saw'st thou good and evil is it spanned –
The crest of contemplation's lonely ridge;
There, whence a myriad tortuous paths go down,
It soars in one bold arch above the earth,
Sweeps o'er the dwindled plains of wealth and dearth,
The oceans of disaster and renown.

Gloomed is the road between the soul and God,
Set beyond vision's reach or thought's assay,
Yet failed it never him who all the way
Held the rope-rail of patience, and had shod

His feet with sureness, nor the lamp did scorn
That his forefathers lit ere he was born.

87

OCTOBER

Now the misty elm-trees stand
Row on row across the vale,
Wardens of a windless land,

By deserted fields, that, pale,
Tell of labour's met demand,
Of heaped ricks and home-travail

Where the steady engine hums:
Now to the still valley comes
Calm of harvest, peace that's knit

Of long weariness, and throws
Softness o'er the tired spirit,
Veils with sleep her worn meadows –

O breeze of our bare hillside,
Sound no more in urgence those
Fresh tales of a world more wide!

THE WATERFALL

(For R. C.)

We traced our river up the rich defiles
That home its tropic flow a hundred miles
From human habitation . . . . Bend on bend,
Each brought the same image – a mirror-end
Curtained by verdure . . . not a hut, a boat,
Broke the lone scene, the silence not a shout,
Plash-song of paddle, grunt of rowlocked oar . . .
Only the tiny flying fish would score
The surface with their flashes, quick as dreams,
Or, rending some deep thicket, shrill as sudden doubt,
The harsh macaws would start us with their haunting screams.

Day after day the muffled pulsings rose
From the hot engine – steadily their dirge
Told our slow passage – till at last the gorge
Steepened, grew barer, seemed about to close,
To block our way . . . we sensed an end, a wall . . . .
Then a roar said: "Behold your goal, the Waterfall". . . .

A thousand feet of torn stream falling sheer
In fog and thunder . . . . Like a theatre
The rocks had taken curve, as, year by year,
The torrent wore at its hard doom-way, inch by inch . . . .
Imagination flew up, then would flinch
From looking down – hung dizzied, even here . . . .

We thought: "God set an awesome gate like this
To cut the low land from the higher land,
As to say: 'Now from valley-loveliness,

From bounded, sheltering beauty, you are banned.' . . . .
There are no wooded cliffs above – there cannot be –
The sky is empty, we can only see
The severing edge from which the river pours;
What lies beyond, or be it heaven or hell,
Is not the world we know . . . . Yet, truly, who can tell
What, after that last arduous portage, may be ours?
What sunny plateau covered with new flowers,
What blest celestial landscape unconfined
To whose blue distances our gleaming way shall wind". . .

Appendix

The following extract from Mrs. Daryush's "Note" in Verses: Fourth Book (1934) *defines her attitude towards syllabics and her practice of syllabic technique.*

The poems without line-capitals are those written in syllabic metres (by which I mean metres governed only by the number of syllables to the line, and in which the number and position of the stresses may be varied at will) and are so printed as a reminder to the reader to follow strictly the natural speech-rhythm, and not to look for stresses where none are intended.

In these metres I make it a rule to allow no elisions except those that are natural, unavoidable, *and complete* in ordinary deliberate speech. (For instance, the semi-vowels before the final consonant in *heaven, chasm,* &c., are only elided when followed by another vowel, and even then only under certain conditions of the speech-rhythm. Such words, therefore, in general, I reckon as disyllables.) In accentual verse the metre demands and justifies the use both of optional and incomplete elisions, but these are obviously out of place in a purely syllabic system. The fact that any ambiguity of this sort would be fatal to it, implies the reduction of the syllabic units to their limit, so as to prevent any uncertainty in the mind of the reader with regard to their further reduction.

I have long thought that on some such system as this for base, it should be possible to build up subtler and more freely-followed accentual patterns than can be obtained either by stress-verse proper, or by the traditional so-called syllabic metres. The bulk of English "syllabic" verse is, of course, not really syllabic in the strict sense, but more truly accentual.